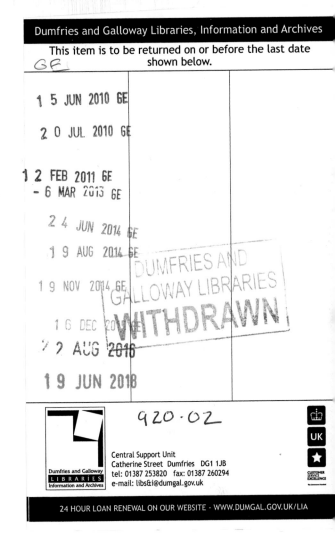

Traitors of the Tower

Alison Weir was born in London, England, and went to the City of London School. Her great love of history started when she read her first novel. Later, she trained as a teacher. She now lives and works in Surrey and her books include *Britain's Royal Families*, *The Six Wives of Henry VIII* and *Mary Queen of Scots and the Murder of Lord Darnley*. She has also published two novels, *Innocent Traitor* and *The Lady Elizabeth*.

Also by Alison Weir

Non-Fiction
Britain's Royal Families: The Complete Genealogy
The Six Wives of Henry VIII
The Princes in the Tower
Lancaster and York: The Wars of the Roses
*Children of England: The Heirs of King Henry VIII
1547–1558*
Elizabeth the Queen
Eleanor of Aquitaine
Henry VIII: King and Court
*Mary Queen of Scots and the Murder of Lord
Darnley*
Isabella: She Wolf of France, Queen of England
*Katherine Swynford: The Story of John of Gaunt
and His Scandalous Duchess*
The Lady in The Tower: The Fall of Anne Boleyn

Fiction
Innocent Traitor
The Lady Elizabeth

Traitors of the
Tower

Alison Weir

VINTAGE BOOKS
London

Published by Vintage 2010

2 4 6 8 10 9 7 5 3 1

Copyright © Alison Weir 2010

Alison Weir has asserted her right under the Copyright, Designs
and Patents Act 1988 to be identified as the author of this work

First published in Great Britain in 2010 by Vintage

Vintage
Random House, 20 Vauxhall Bridge Road,
London SW1V 2SA

www.vintage-books.co.uk

Addresses for companies within The Random House Group Limited
can be found at: www.randomhouse.co.uk/offices.htm

The Random House Group Limited Reg. No. 954009

A CIP catalogue record for this book
is available from the British Library

ISBN 9780099542285

The Random House Group Limited supports The Forest Stewardship
Council (FSC), the leading international forest certification
organisation. All our titles that are printed on Greenpeace
approved FSC certified paper carry the FSC logo. Our
paper procurement policy can be found at:
www.rbooks.co.uk/environment

Printed and bound in Great Britain by
CPI Bookmarque, Croydon CR0 4TD

Contents

Introduction

In the Tower of London, between 1483 and 1601, seven famous traitors lost their heads. Visitors are often drawn to the scaffold site on Tower Green where they are said to have died. In fact, five were put to death in a different place within the Tower, in front of what is now the Waterloo Barracks.

This book tells the grim and tragic stories of the traitors who died in the Tower.

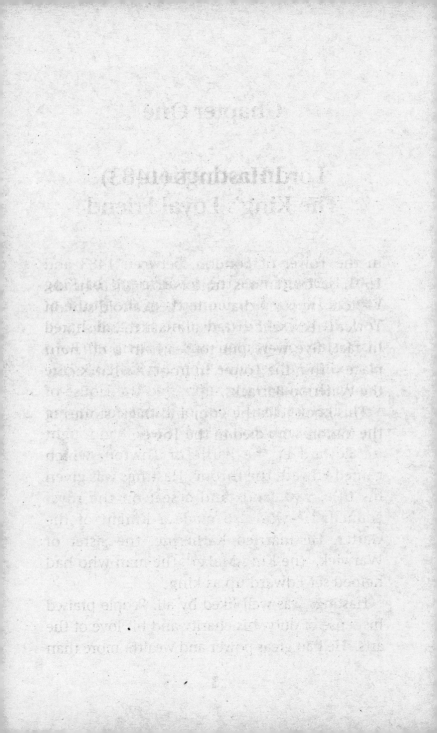

Chapter One

Lord Hastings (1483)
The King's Loyal Friend

Chapter One

Lord Hastings (1483)
The King's Loyal Friend

Lord Hastings was the loyal friend of King Edward IV, the first monarch of the House of York. He helped Edward all his life, and shared his tastes for women and good food. Born around 1431, he came from a good Yorkshire family that had long supported the House of York against the House of Lancaster during the Wars of the Roses. In 1461 he had fought for Edward at the Battle of Towton, which gained Edward the throne. Hastings was given his title, vast lands and a seat on the royal council. He was also made a Knight of the Garter. He married Katherine, the sister of Warwick, 'the King-Maker', the man who had helped set Edward up as king.

Hastings was well liked by all. People praised his sense of duty, his charity and his love of the arts. He had great power and wealth, more than

3

many of higher rank, and people only got to see the King with Hastings' favour. But his power, and his wenching with the King, earned him the hatred of the Queen, Elizabeth Wydeville. Her family were his rivals for royal favour, and his deadly foes. Hastings was also rivals with Lord Dorset, the Queen's elder son, for the love of Elizabeth Shore, the King's mistress.

In April 1483, Edward IV died at the early age of forty-one. On his deathbed, he ordered Hastings, the Queen and Dorset to make peace, which they made a show of doing. Edward's son and heir was just twelve years old, so in his will he named his brother, Richard, Duke of Gloucester, as Lord Protector while the boy was too young to rule. But Gloucester was in the north, and after Edward had died, the Queen tried to seize power. Hastings was well aware that she might now take revenge on him, but his main concern was for the new young King, Edward V.

Edward V was then at Ludlow Castle on the Welsh border. As Prince of Wales, he had been learning how to rule his subjects. The Queen sent for him to come to London at once to be crowned. She wanted a great army to escort him, but Hastings thought this might provoke trouble and bloodshed. He won the day with threats against the Queen's family, the Wydevilles, and so only a small escort went with the young King.

Gloucester too feared the Wydevilles, who had not told him of his brother's death. He learned of it from Hastings, who also wrote that the Queen meant to remove him from power. He told Gloucester to hurry to London with a strong force of men , and to take Edward V into his care on the way. Hastings added that he himself was in danger from the Queen's party, and he could not wait for Gloucester to reach London.

Gloucester, wearing black for his brother, rode south at once with three hundred men. At Northampton, he met up with his ally, the Duke of Buckingham, and a large force. In London, Hastings told the royal council that the humble blood of the Queen and her family made them unfit to rule, and that Gloucester should govern the realm. This earned him no credit with the Wydevilles.

At Stony Stratford, Gloucester and Buckingham met up with Edward V and his escort, which was led by Earl Rivers, the Queen's brother, and her younger son, Sir Richard Grey. Gloucester and Buckingham seized the King, arrested Rivers and Grey, who were put in prison, and then rode on to London with a very shocked Edward V.

The power of the Wydevilles had been broken at a stroke. The Queen, in great fear, now took sanctuary in Westminster Abbey with her younger son, Richard, Duke of York, and her five daughters. Hastings sent a message to assure her that all would be well, but she did not believe it. He had done his best to destroy her, she said.

London was in an uproar. Hastings tried to restore calm by telling the council that Gloucester had been faithful to the dead King, Edward IV, and would now be true to Edward's son. He had only arrested Rivers and Grey for his own safety. In saying this, Hastings turned many people against the Wydevilles. But there were some on the council who were wary of Gloucester's cunning.

Soon after arriving in London, Gloucester was in complete control of the young King and the country. He got rid of the Queen's friends on the council, and sent Edward V to live in the palace in the Tower of London. The Tower was not yet known as a prison. Edward IV had held court there many times, and it was usual for a king to spend the days before his crowning at the Tower.

Hastings was pleased to see Gloucester in charge, and keen to do all he could for him. He showed much joy at this 'new world', which had been won without one drop of blood being shed.

But Gloucester knew he would never be safe. The young King was his mother's son, and it would only be a matter of time before he turned on his uncle. For his own safety, Gloucester had to make a bid for the throne itself. Some people thought he had plotted that all along.

Hastings was now part of Edward V's small court in the Tower, helping the boy to learn how to rule. It was perhaps at this time that the young King gave him the fine book known as 'The Hastings Hours', which is now in the British Library in London. Gloucester kept Hastings in the important positions he had held under Edward IV, but there was no reward for helping him gain power. Gloucester 'loved him well', but he liked and trusted Buckingham more. He knew that Hastings was deeply loyal to Edward V, and would block any move to depose him. In Gloucester's mind Hastings was now an enemy.

On the face of it, all seemed well. Hastings had no reason to doubt Gloucester. But Lord Stanley, who did not trust Gloucester, warned him to be careful. Then Buckingham sounded out Hastings on how he would act if Gloucester claimed the throne. Hastings used 'terrible words', saying he would accept him as Protector for Edward V, but never as king – and sealed his own doom.

Hastings was alarmed to learn that Gloucester was aiming for the crown. He may have warned Edward V of what was afoot. He sought help from other lords of the council. He spoke of seizing the King by force and removing Gloucester. He even tried to gain the support of the Queen, though she had no power to help. But before Hastings could act, Gloucester found out what was going on. He chose to believe that Hastings was plotting his death. He needed to make a case for getting rid of this upright man who stood in his way. As one writer put it, he 'rushed headlong into crime'.

On 10 June 1483, Gloucester wrote to powerful people in the city of York asking for aid against the Queen's family and friends. There can be no doubt that he was thinking of Hastings. He added that these people 'daily do intend to murder and destroy us and the old royal blood of this realm'. He then sent orders for Rivers and Grey to be put to death, 'so as to leave no danger to himself from any quarter'.

Three days later, Hastings was among those called by Gloucester to a council meeting in the

Tower of London. They thought they had been brought there to discuss the crowning of Edward V. Gloucester arrived smiling, and chatted with the lords in a friendly manner. After asking the Bishop of Ely to send him some fruit from his garden, he left them to debate state matters. But he had laid his plans with care and cunning.

An hour or so later, Gloucester came back, in an angry mood. He was 'frowning, fretting and biting his lips'. He sat silent for a while, then glared at Hastings.

'What do men deserve for plotting the death of me?' he asked. Hastings said that if they had done such a wicked thing, they were worthy of just punishment.

'If?' cried Gloucester in a fury, rising to his feet. 'I tell you, they have done it, and I will make good upon your body, traitor!' He then accused four other men in the room of being traitors to him, even though crimes against a lord protector were not in fact treason. He said they had plotted with the Queen against his rule and his life. A later tale had him crying that the Queen and Elizabeth Shore had caused his arm to wither by using witchcraft, but there is no proof that he had a withered arm. He did shout that an ambush had been set to trap him.

His victims had no chance to reply. Armed guards had been hiding in the next room, and when Gloucester banged his hand on the table, they burst in, yelling, 'Treason!' There was a sharp scuffle, which ended in the arrest of Hastings and four others.

Gloucester told Hastings he had better see a priest at once and confess his sins, 'for I will not dine until I see your head off!' Hastings realised he was going to die within minutes. There was no trial, and there can be no doubt that Gloucester was acting outside the law. It was the right of a lord to be tried by his fellows, but Gloucester dared not risk a trial because Hastings knew too much about his plot to seize the throne. In fact, this was the start of Gloucester's rule by terror.

He paid no heed to Hastings' pleas for mercy. Nor did Buckingham, whom Gloucester put in charge of the doomed man. A priest was summoned, but was not allowed much time to give the last rites. Then Hastings was dragged by an usher to 'the green beside the chapel in the Tower'. There he was made to kneel by a block of wood left by some workmen, and an usher struck off his head with a sword. Edward may even have been watching, for the windows of his rooms faced Tower Green.

'Thus fell Hastings, killed not by those enemies he had always feared, but by a friend whom he had never doubted.' And so Edward V lost his best friend. People were sad and shocked to hear of Hastings' death. When Rivers and Grey too were killed without trial, and the little Duke of York was forced to join his brother in the Tower, they woke up to the fact that Gloucester was bent on taking the throne.

Without the loyal Hastings to defend him, Edward V was declared a bastard and deposed. He and his brother, the two 'Princes in the Tower', were never seen again. On 26 June 1483, less than two weeks after Hastings died, Gloucester became king, as Richard III.

Hastings was buried in the fine chantry chapel built for him in St George's Chapel at Windsor, near the last resting place of his great friend, King Edward IV. His tomb can still be seen there today.

Chapter Two

Queen Anne Boleyn (1536)
'I Have a Little Neck'

On 29 January 1536, Anne Boleyn, Henry VIII's second wife, lost a baby son, born dead after four months. This was her fourth child, but the only one still living was a girl, Elizabeth, born in 1533. In Tudor times, no one thought a woman might be a powerful ruler, as Elizabeth later was, and the King had long wanted a son to succeed him on the throne. Now, to his 'great distress', that son had been born dead.

Henry VIII had hoped for a boy from his first wife, Katherine of Aragon, but of her six children, all had died young except a daughter, Mary. By 1526, the King had fallen madly in love with her lady-in-waiting, Anne Boleyn. Anne had dark hair and eyes, and she was clever and witty. Henry wrote ardent love letters to her, and begged her to be his mistress, but she kept him at bay, holding out for marriage.

In 1527, Henry asked the Pope to end his marriage to Katherine. But the Pope did not want to offend Katherine's mighty nephew, the Emperor Charles V, so he held back. After six years of waiting in vain for the Pope to speak, Henry broke with the Church of Rome and made himself Head of the Church of England. In 1533, he married Anne and had his union with Katherine declared null and void. By then, he was forty-two and his need for a son was urgent.

But in the three years that followed his secret wedding to Anne Boleyn, Henry was not a kind husband. His 'blind passion' had not lasted, and he had turned to other women, telling Anne to 'shut her eyes as her betters had done'. Now he was chasing after her maid, Jane Seymour, and Anne had borne a dead son. Yet it does not seem that the loss of her child was the main cause of her downfall. She was hated by the people, and by many at court, who were doing their best to get rid of her.

Chief among them was Henry's minister, Thomas Cromwell, who was 'ready at all things, evil or good'. Clever and ruthless, he was 'the King's ear and mind'. Cromwell had once been

Anne's friend, but they had fallen out. She did not agree with him on many things, and feared that his growing power was a threat to her. They were now rivals, and she had even said 'she would see his head cut off'.

Anne's downfall has long been seen as the result of a failed marriage. It is often thought that Henry VIII had tired of her and asked Cromwell to make a case for getting rid of her. Yet it seems that it was Cromwell, not Henry, who was the man behind her overthrow.

Cromwell was later to admit that 'he had thought up and plotted the affair'. He had good reason: Anne had regained the King's favour, and had made it clear to all that 'wicked ministers' should be hanged. This came at a time when Cromwell had angered Henry. Plainly, he feared it would be his neck, or hers.

Cromwell built his case on the King's fear of treason and the Queen's teasing nature. Anne had failed to give the King a son. She had proved unfit to be a queen, with her temper and her moods. She was hated by the people, and Catholics did not see her as the King's true wife. More to the point, she was known to enjoy flirting with the men in her circle. For years there had been lewd gossip about her. It would not be hard for people to believe that a woman who had slept with the King before their marriage could have affairs after it.

Cromwell quizzed many who knew Anne, and found evidence against her. We know very little about it, but he was able to build a strong case. It seems that Cromwell showed Henry VIII things he could not ignore.

On 2 May 1536, Anne was arrested for treason at Greenwich Palace and taken by barge to the Tower of London. Entering the Tower, she was in a frail state. She 'fell down on her knees', begging God to help her 'as she was not guilty'. She knew it was rare for anyone accused of treason to escape death.

Sir William Kingston, the Constable of the Tower, led her away.

'Mr Kingston, do I go into a dungeon?' Anne asked.

Kingston told her no, she would be held in the Queen's Lodgings in the palace.

'It is too good for me!' Anne cried. 'Jesu, have mercy on me!'

In her gilded prison, Anne veered from tears to laughter. She could not believe that the King meant her any real harm. She was well treated, but four ladies had been set to spy on her and report all she said. In her distress, she made some very suspect remarks that would be used against her.

While Anne was in the Tower, the King would not see anyone or appear in public. Yet he was seen sailing along the Thames in his barge at night, with ladies by his side and music playing. He had his new love, Jane Seymour, brought to a house by the river and he visited her there. She was now as richly dressed and treated as if she were queen already.

At dinner with a bishop, Henry told the guests that he had seen all this coming, and believed that more than a hundred men had slept with Anne. One envoy wrote, 'You never saw a prince or husband make greater show of his horns.'

A week after Anne's arrest, two lists of charges were drawn up against her, accusing her of adultery with five men. Three were friends of the King, while one, Mark Smeaton, was a lute player. That was shocking enough, but the fifth man was Anne's own brother, George Boleyn, Lord Rochford. His wife, Jane, Lady Rochford, had given so-called 'proof' of incest. It seemed George Boleyn had once been alone with Anne and that he had kissed her. Anne was also said to have plotted the King's death so that she could marry one of her lovers and rule England with him.

Only Smeaton pleaded guilty. Anne and the rest would maintain their innocence. But on 12 May, all the men except George Boleyn were tried in Westminster Hall and condemned to death.

Three days later, at a show trial in the great hall of the Tower, watched by three thousand people, the Queen was tried by twenty-six lords. Her own father seems to have been among them. Never before had a queen of England been brought to trial. It caused a great stir, and much scandal.

Anne was calm and composed. She showed no fear. She put up a strong defence, causing some to say that the trial was just an excuse to get rid of her, but it did her no good. When the lords were asked for their verdict, all said: 'Guilty.'

A hush fell as Anne's uncle, the Duke of Norfolk, weeping, told her she was to be 'burnt here within the Tower, or else to have thy head cut off', as the King should decide. When Anne heard these dread words, she was calm. She said, 'O Father, Thou who art the way, the life and the truth, know whether I have deserved this death.' She added that she was ready to die, but very sorry that others, blameless as she, should die because of her. She swore that she had always been true to the King, but admitted that she had been a proud and jealous wife. 'But God knows that I have not sinned against him in any other way.' She asked only for time to prepare her soul for death.

Anne was taken back to the Queen's Lodgings, where she spent her last days. It is often claimed that she was held in two Tudor rooms in the Queen's House facing Tower Green, but they date from the early 1540s, after her death. The ladies who had spied on her were sent away, and four young maids took their places. They were known to Anne, and kind to her.

The Queen's brother, George Boleyn, was tried after her, and he too was found guilty. All five men were beheaded on Tower Hill on 17 May. Anne was made to watch them die from a window in the Tower. That same day, with her consent, her marriage to Henry VIII was dissolved, and her daughter Elizabeth made a bastard.

'Moved by pity', the King allowed his wife the kinder death. Even before her trial, he had sent to France for an expert swordsman to behead her. This proves he had never meant to have her burned at the stake. There can be little doubt that the hope of a quick death by the sword was used to gain her consent to the ending of her marriage.

The Queen was to die at nine o'clock on 18 May, but Cromwell needed time to make sure that a good crowd would be there to watch. Justice must be seen to be done. But the delay was torture for Anne.

'Master Kingston,' she said to the Constable, 'I hear say I shall not die afore noon, and I am very sorry for it, for I thought then to be dead and past my pain.' When Kingston told her there should be no pain, she said, 'I have a little neck.' Then she put her hand about it, laughing. Kingston wrote: 'I have seen many men and also women put to death, and all have been in great sorrow, but this lady has much joy and pleasure in death.'

At noon, her beheading was delayed again, until the next morning. Again, Anne begged that the King might hasten her end, as she was ready to die and feared she might lose her nerve. But her pleas fell on deaf ears.

That day, she made her peace with God, stating that she had never offended with her body against the King. It is hard to believe she would have put her soul at risk when she was about to face her Maker.

Anne spent much of her last night praying. At

eight o'clock on the morning of 19 May 1536, attended by the four young ladies, she was led by Sir William Kingston to a new scaffold that had been built for her. Draped in black, it stood before the 'House of Ordnance' (now the Waterloo Barracks), facing the White Tower in the Tower of London. A thousand people had come to watch Anne die. They saw her mount the steps, wearing a rich grey robe with a white fur cape and a gable hood. She was calm and brave, and made a short speech.

She said 'she was come to die, as she was judged by the law. She would accuse none, nor say anything of why she was judged. She prayed for the King, and called him a most gentle prince. If any would meddle with her cause, she asked them to judge the best. And so she took her leave of them, and of the world', and asked them all to pray for her.

There was no block. She knelt upright on the straw, bound her eyes, and then prayed aloud as she waited for the blow, saying over and over again, 'Oh, Lord God have pity on my soul!' The headsman took off his shoes, came up behind her, swung his sword, and took off her head 'at a stroke'. Her eyes and lips were seen to move as the head fell.

'The Queen died boldly,' Sir William

Kingston wrote. Her ladies, weeping, wrapped the head and body in white cloths. No one had thought to provide a coffin, and in the end an arrow chest was all that could be found. Anne's body was buried that day in the royal chapel of St Peter in Chains in the Tower, before the altar. Ten days later, the King married Jane Seymour.

Without any real proof of Anne's guilt, and with her having been judged only on weak and false evidence, there can be little doubt that she went to her death an innocent woman.

Chapter Three

Margaret Pole, Countess of Salisbury (1541) Hacked to Death

Margaret was the daughter of the Duke of Clarence, the younger brother of King Edward IV. Born near Bath in 1473, she was a princess of the House of York. She and her younger brother, Edward, Earl of Warwick, grew up in a rich household, but their childhood was marred by sadness. In 1476, when Margaret was three, her mother died in childbirth. The baby did not long outlive her.

Margaret's father, the Duke of Clarence, was not trusted by his brother, Edward IV, and with good reason. Some years before, he had turned traitor and tried to depose Edward. He had allied with the King's enemies and driven him from England. When Edward regained his throne, they had made peace, but Clarence was still jealous of his brother and hated the Queen. In

1477, he accused her of the murder of his wife, saying she had given her poison. He also said in public that the King was a bastard. There was no truth in all this, but the Queen feared that Clarence was a threat to her and her children. Edward could not let Clarence get away with such insults, so he sent him to the Tower.

Clarence was charged with high treason and brought before the House of Lords, where Edward himself sat in judgement on him. Thus it was that one brother condemned the other to death. Their mother begged the King for mercy. Most traitors were hanged, drawn, beheaded and cut in quarters, but Clarence was a lord and it was the right of lords to be beheaded.

In the end, Edward let Clarence choose how he would die. It is said he was drowned in a butt of Malmsey wine. His daughter Margaret would always wear a wine barrel jewel at her wrist in memory of him, and this can be seen in her portrait at the National Portrait Gallery in London.

Margaret and her brother Warwick were sent to Sheen Palace to be brought up with the King's children. When Richard III seized power in 1483, they were moved with other young royals to Sheriff Hutton Castle in Yorkshire.

There they lived in great state and were well looked after.

After the death of Richard III's only son in 1484, young Warwick was next in line for the throne, but Richard did not name him his heir. This might have been because Warwick was slow-witted. But Richard III knew that Warwick had a good claim to the throne, so he kept close watch on him. He feared that others might take up his cause, for he, Richard, was not well liked.

In 1485, Henry Tudor led an army into England and defeated and killed Richard III at the Battle of Bosworth. Henry then had himself crowned Henry VII, the first king of the House of Tudor. Henry was aware that Warwick had a better claim to the throne than he did, so he shut him up in the Tower of London. The poor boy was to spend the rest of his sad life there.

Over the next few years, two pretenders, Lambert Simnel and Perkin Warbeck, claimed to be Warwick, in the hope of becoming king. This made Henry VII realise that the simple young man posed a real danger to him. In 1499, he placed agents in the Tower who led Warwick to plot treason with Perkin Warbeck. This gave Henry VII the excuse he needed to have Warwick beheaded, and Warbeck hanged.

In these years, Margaret had grown up to be pious and learned. In 1494, she had married Sir Richard Pole. Henry VII's mother was Sir Richard's aunt. Sir Richard served Henry VII well, and was given high offices at court and in Wales in return. He was also made a Knight of the Garter. Margaret bore him four sons and a daughter before he died in 1505.

Things got better for Margaret after Henry VIII came to the throne in 1509. He was always wary of those with royal blood, fearing they would plot against him, but he liked her, and did not doubt that she was loyal to him. He called her 'the most saintly woman in England'. He wanted to make up to her for the unjust death of her brother, Warwick. He gave her a good income, and in 1513 made her Countess of Salisbury, a title that had belonged to her father. He also paid for her clever son, Reginald, to go to Oxford University, and set him on the way to a career in the Church.

Margaret was now a rich woman with vast lands. She was often at court, and became close friends with Henry's first wife, Katherine of Aragon. Katherine had always felt guilt about the death of Margaret's brother. Her parents, the King and Queen of Spain, had seen Warwick as a threat to the Tudors, and would not let her come to England until he was dead. She always said that her marriage had been made in blood, but it is clear that Margaret did not hold this against her.

By 1519, Margaret was serving as governess to Katherine's daughter, the Princess Mary. Margaret was her godmother. Margaret and the Queen both hoped at one time that Mary would marry Margaret's son, Reginald Pole, and unite the Houses of York and Tudor, but the King had other plans. When Mary, aged nine, was given her own court at Ludlow Castle in 1525, Margaret went with her. She took the place of Mary's mother, and made sure she stayed healthy and worked hard at her lessons.

Two years later, after Henry VIII made it clear that he wanted to end his marriage to Queen Katherine and marry Anne Boleyn, Margaret Pole stood by Katherine. She and her family hated Anne, and Reginald spoke out hotly against her. In the end, he had to flee to Italy to escape the King's wrath. There, he rose high in the Church, and was made a cardinal. Many years later, Henry's daughter, Mary, would make him Archbishop of Canterbury.

For years, Margaret helped Katherine to shelter Mary from her parents' troubles. When Katherine was no longer allowed to see Mary after 1531, Margaret was there for the princess, giving her support and kindness. But in 1533, after Henry had married Anne Boleyn and divorced Katherine, he tried to make Mary accept Anne as queen. Mary would not. When Margaret Pole refused to give up Mary's jewels, Henry had her removed from her post. Margaret told him she would still follow and serve the Princess at her own expense, but Henry sent her away.

Margaret was out of favour for three years. But after Anne Boleyn's downfall, the King married Jane Seymour, and Margaret was again made welcome at court. The people cheered when they saw this 'lady of honour and virtue' arrive. They knew she was Mary's governess and that she had stood up for her and for the former Queen, Katherine, and they loved her for that. But she would not stay in favour for long.

In 1536, Henry asked Reginald Pole to write down his views on his marriages. He knew that if he could gain Pole's support, the Catholic world would look more kindly on him. Safe in Italy, Pole could not resist writing just what he thought of the King and Anne Boleyn. His book caused deep offence to the King. It was nothing less than treason, and it really damned Reginald Pole in Henry's eyes. From now on, Henry was filled with hatred for Pole. It was clear that Pole could never return to England while Henry lived.

In much distress, Margaret spoke out against the book. She said she wished she had never given birth to such a traitor. She wrote to her son, attacking him strongly, and sent the letter to the King's council first. It was all in vain, for Henry knew that her views were the same as Pole's. 'The King will kill us all,' her other sons warned.

Henry never forgot Reginald Pole's treason. He had the family watched. He was all too aware that royal blood ran in their veins. He told one envoy that he would destroy them.

In August 1538, Henry sent one of Margaret's younger sons, Geoffrey, to the Tower for aiding his exiled brother, Reginald. Geoffrey Pole, in great fear, blurted out something about a plot. It seems there had been something of the kind, inept and half-hearted, but it was made out that the Poles and their friends had plotted to kill the King.

Later that year, the King had Margaret's eldest son, Henry Pole, Lord Montagu, arrested, along with his cousin, the Marquess of Exeter. Both were beheaded. There was a round-up of other family members, and even the children were sent to prison in the Tower.

Margaret Pole's castle at Warblington in Hampshire had been searched. A white silk tunic had been found, bearing the royal arms of a king. Only a monarch might bear such arms. Margaret firmly denied that she had ever meant to dispute the right of Henry VIII to the throne, but this did not save her.

Henry deeply feared that Margaret Pole might be the focus of a revolt against the Crown. In March 1539, she too was taken to the Tower, where she was put in a cold cell. She had no warm clothes and was given only poor food to eat.

Margaret was not given a chance to defend herself. In May, she was condemned to lose her life and her goods. The King took all her lands, but he did not send her to the scaffold. She was sixty-five, so he may have thought she would die soon anyway. She lay in the Tower for two years, weak and cold. Then in spring 1541, Katherine Howard, Henry's fifth wife, took pity on her. She sent her a furred nightgown, shoes, slippers, stockings and other items of warm clothing.

A few weeks later, there was a revolt in Yorkshire against Henry VIII's rule. The King, as ever, feared a plot to depose him and put someone else on the throne. He recalled that

Margaret Pole still lived, and that her sons were traitors. She had had nothing to do with the revolt, but he chose to see her as a threat to his safety. In spite of the Queen's pleas, he ordered that the death sentence be carried out.

On the morning of 28 May 1541, the aged Countess was woken by the Constable of the Tower and told she was to die that day. She told him that she was guilty of no crime. He gave her a short time to prepare her soul for death, then led her out to Tower Green. There the Lord Mayor of London and others were waiting to watch her die. She walked bravely to her death, commended her soul to God, and asked all present to pray for the King, the Queen and her god-daughter Mary.

There was no scaffold, just a low block. It is not true that Margaret Pole refused to lay her head on it, crying, 'So should traitors do, but I am none!' Nor did the hangman chase her around the scaffold with the axe. These are later stories. But her end was bloody. She did lie down on the block, but the hangman was new to his job and not skilled at cutting off heads. Faced with this great lady, he began to panic, and struck out blindly, hacking at her head, neck and shoulders until she was dead.

The cruel end of Margaret Pole shocked even

the Tudor court, but the King showed no sorrow. It did not matter to him that he was now more feared than beloved by his subjects.

Margaret was buried in the chapel in the Tower, near Anne Boleyn. The fine tomb she had had built for herself in Christchurch Priory, Dorset, can still be seen today, but it is empty. The Catholic Church now honours her as a martyr, and calls her 'Blessed Margaret Pole'.

Chapter Four

Queen Katherine Howard
(1542)
'Rose Without a Thorn'

Katherine Howard was one of the most tragic queens in history. Married young to the ill and obese Henry VIII, as his fifth wife, she was ill-fitted in nearly every way for her royal rank. She was to pay a high price for her failings.

The exact date of Katherine's birth is not known. It was between 1519 and 1525. Her father was a poor younger son of the noble Howard family. Her mother had died when Katherine was a child, and Katherine was brought up in Norfolk by her grandmother, the Duchess of Norfolk. The Duchess was guilty of neglect, and Katherine was badly taught and left to run wild.

Katherine was a small girl, slim and pretty, with brown hair. She had a kind heart and was easily led. She was very young when her music master, Henry Manox, tried to seduce her. He would later boast that he knew of a secret mole on her body and had felt her private parts. Before he had got any further, the Duchess walked in on the pair. Shocked, she beat them both, and put an end to their love play.

But she then seems to have left Katherine to do as she pleased. Katherine shared a bedchamber with female servants and distant relatives. She saw, and took part in, the games with men that took place there. Before long, she fell in love with a cousin, Francis Dereham, and was soon sleeping naked with her lover.

The other women quickly worked out what all the 'puffing and blowing' behind the bedcurtains meant. Some were quite shocked. Things got to the stage where the young couple were calling each other 'husband' and 'wife' in front of others. In Tudor times, this was taken as a contract between them, which was as binding as a marriage, and could only be set aside by the Church.

The Duchess was not aware of all these goings-on. Soon, Dereham went to Ireland to seek his fortune. He had vowed to come back and claim Katherine as his bride. But then the Duchess moved her household to London.

It was 1540, and Henry VIII had just married

his fourth wife, the German Anne of Cleves; Henry was not attracted to his bride, and would not sleep with her. Instead, he had his advisers running round in circles trying to find a way to end the marriage.

Katherine Howard's uncle, Thomas Howard, Duke of Norfolk, was the leading Catholic peer at court. He and his friends were keen to see Anne removed. They did not want the King coming under the influence of the church reformers who had arranged her marriage. They wanted a Catholic queen.

Norfolk saw his niece, pretty Katherine Howard, waiting on Anne of Cleeves. It came to him that she would be the perfect wife for the King. This was not the first time that Norfolk had plotted to put a niece on the throne. He had been uncle to Anne Boleyn, but his hopes of greatness had been dashed when Anne was beheaded. But Katherine, the Duchess told him, was no Anne Boleyn: she was a good girl.

Norfolk did his best to make the King notice Katherine, and his efforts soon bore fruit. By April 1540, Henry VIII had fallen so much in love with her that he could not keep his hands off her. Backed by her family, Katherine led him on. Henry made her grants of land, and it seems she wanted to be queen. But she was no Anne

Boleyn. She was much younger and far more empty-headed. She had no idea that her past would come back to haunt her.

As soon as Henry VIII had got rid of Anne of Cleves, he married Katherine. The wedding took place in July 1540 at the palace of Oatlands in Surrey. Then the royal couple spent ten days alone in private.

Henry was then forty-nine, very fat, and old for his years. But he was given a new lease of life by his young bride. He loaded her with gifts, petted her in public and showed all the signs of being in love with her. He could not do enough for her. In tribute to his love, she took the motto: 'No other will than his.'

Katherine enjoyed her new riches, the great palaces, the dancing, the fine gowns, the bright jewels and the sweet little lapdogs. Whether she was as pleased with her fat and ailing husband is not known. Rumours that Henry was impotent had been going round since Anne Boleyn's downfall, but they may not have been true. Katherine also had to put up with the stink of his leg ulcers.

Henry was happy in his marriage. He thought himself blessed. He believed he had found the wife of his dreams. He struck a gold medal on which Katherine was called his 'rose without a thorn'. He thanked God for sending him such a 'perfect jewel'. The whole realm was made to 'do her honour'.

Henry still hoped for an heir, and in April 1541, Katherine thought she was pregnant, but it seems she was not. It was as well, in view of what was to come.

Silly Katherine had taken some of the Duchess's servants into her household, those same servants who had seen her romping with Dereham. At least one seems to have got in by the threat of blackmail. Katherine even took Dereham on to work for her. Her love for him had cooled, though, and by the spring of 1541, she had begun a secret affair with Thomas Culpeper, her cousin. He was a member of the King's Privy Chamber, and much liked by Henry.

Taking risks with Culpeper was a stupid thing to do, given the fate of Anne Boleyn. But Katherine seems to have been heedless of the danger. Nor did she show much wisdom in falling for this young man, who had raped the wife of a park-keeper while his friends held her down. Then he had killed a man who had seen it all and vowed to report him. Culpeper had got away with it just because the King was so fond of him.

Lady Rochford was one of these who had served

the Queen. She was the widow of Anne Boleyn's brother; it was she who had accused her husband and his sister of incest. Now she aided Katherine's affair with Culpeper, keeping watch when they met in secret.

When Henry took Katherine on a long journey to the north of England in the autumn of 1541, the lovers met as often as they could, even in a privy. Katherine would always 'seek for the back doors and the back stairs herself'. Once, when the King came to sleep with his wife, he was kept waiting outside her door while Lady Rochford got rid of Culpeper. Katherine was putting herself in grave danger.

Katherine's past was revealed when Mary Hall, one of the Duchess's servants, told Thomas Cranmer, the Archbishop of Canterbury, about it. Cranmer was only too willing to bring down the Catholic Queen Katherine. He wrote a letter to the King, setting down what he had heard, and left it in the royal pew, so that Henry would find it when he went to Mass. Henry read it, but did not believe it could be true. He asked Cranmer to find out more.

When sound proof of Katherine's shameless deeds was shown to Henry, he broke down in public and called for a sword to kill her. Then he ordered her arrest, and that of Lady Rochford.

Katherine was shut in her rooms at Hampton Court and told that it was 'no more the time to dance'. Legend has it that she broke free of her guards and ran to plead with Henry at the door of the Chapel Royal. It was said she knew that, if she could once more use her charms on him, he would forgive her. But she was dragged away, screaming, before she could reach him.

Henry left Hampton Court a broken and aged man. Katherine would never see him again. It was said that he looked 'old and grey after the mishap of the Queen'. He tried to soothe his grief by going hunting and eating rich food. He was now so fat that three men could fit into his clothes. A new law was passed making it treason for a woman to marry the King without first telling him if she had a past. One wit wrote, 'Few, if any, ladies at court would aspire to such an honour.'

Thomas Cranmer, the Archbishop of Canterbury, questioned the Queen and her servants for many days. Katherine was in a crazed state, and at first denied it all, even that she had been as good as married to Dereham. Admitting that might have helped her, for it would have made her marriage to the King null and void. But the foolish girl thought that denying everything was safer.

In the end, she broke down and confessed what had taken place before her marriage. That was no crime, of course. But Dereham let slip that she had left him for Culpeper, and adultery was another matter. In a queen, it was high treason. Katherine would only admit that she had flirted with Culpeper, given him gifts and called him her 'little sweet fool'. Yes, she had sent him a letter ending with the words, 'Yours as long as life endures', but she firmly denied she had ever slept with him. She accused Lady Rochford of spreading that rumour, but Lady Rochford would not admit it.

Culpeper was arrested. He said he had met the Queen in secret many times, but that they had not 'passed beyond words'. But when the council were told that they had met in the privy, they believed the worst.

Katherine was doomed. Her servants were sent away. Her jewels were given back to the King. She was sent to Syon Abbey by the Thames, where she was well looked after but made to live quietly and dress in sober clothes. Her rich gowns and jewels had been taken from her. The Howard family fell from favour, and many of its members were sent to prison. Dereham and Culpeper were tried and beheaded.

Katherine did not face trial. Instead, the

House of Lords condemned her as a traitor, who must forfeit her life and goods. Three months after her arrest, the lords came for her. This was when she realised that the King really did mean to have her put to death and, in panic, she refused to go with them. But they forced her into the barge, and took her to the Tower. They passed under London Bridge, where the rotting heads of Dereham and Culpeper had been set on spikes.

In the Tower, Katherine could not stop weeping. Then she calmed down and asked if the block could be brought to her, so that she could practise how to behave nobly at her death, to uphold the honour of the great Howard family. She went to the scaffold on 13 February 1542, so weak with fear that she could hardly stand. She told the crowd that she deserved a hundred deaths. Then she knelt, and the axe took off her head with one blow. Wrapped in a black blanket, she was buried near her cousin, Anne Boleyn, in the Tower chapel.

Chapter Five

Jane Parker, Lady Rochford
(1542)
The 'Wicked Wife'

The claim that incest had taken place between Anne Boleyn and her brother, Lord Rochford, was said to have been made by his own wife, Jane, Lady Rochford. She helped bring to ruin not only her husband and his sister, but also Katherine Howard. Hers is one of the darker tales of the traitors of the Tower.

Jane Parker was the daughter of Henry, Lord Morley; her mother was a distant cousin of the King. She had been 'brought up in the court' from a young age, and was a maid of honour to Katherine of Aragon. In 1520, she had gone with Queen Katherine to 'the Field of Cloth of Gold', the famous meeting between Henry VIII and the King of France. Jane had become one of the court's young stars, and in 1522 she danced the role of 'Constancy' in a display with Anne Boleyn and others.

By the end of 1524, Jane had married George Boleyn. As a wedding gift, the King gave the couple a manor in Norfolk. The Boleyn family went up in the world after Henry VIII began courting George's sister, Anne Boleyn. George Boleyn became one of the most powerful men at court, loaded with offices and wealth, and in 1529 he became Lord Rochford.

Lady Rochford was for years a member of Anne Boleyn's circle, and from 1533 she served her as a lady-in-waiting. At Anne's crowning that year, Jane was given a special place with many great ladies.

An usher of the court, George Cavendish, who knew Jane but had no love for the Boleyns, took a poor view of her. He wrote that she had been brought up without a bridle, and left to follow her lust and filthy pleasure, wasting her youth. She had no respect for her marriage vows, and did not fear God.

Lady Rochford had a talent for plotting. She was to prove that over and over again. In October 1534, when Henry VIII was unfaithful to Anne Boleyn, Anne asked Jane to help her get rid of the King's mistress. The plan was to replace his mistress with Madge Shelton, the

Queen's cousin, who would not be so much of a threat to Anne. But Henry found out, and Lady Rochford was dismissed from her post of lady-in-waiting and sent away from court. We do not know when, or if, she returned.

In October 1535, while the King and Queen were away on a tour of the kingdom, Mary, Henry VIII's daughter by his first wife, was seen in public. She was popular, and many felt sorry for the way she had been treated.

To show their support, 'a vast crowd of women, unknown to their husbands, came before her, weeping and crying that she was their true princess'. It was treason to say this, and their leaders were put in prison in the Tower. One of them was Lady Rochford. She does not appear to have been in prison there for long.

It has been said that speaking out in favour of Mary was surprising for Lady Rochford, when she knew her future lay with the Boleyns. But quite a few of their party had given up on them, put off by Anne's pride and sharp words. It also seems that Lady Rochford was jealous of her husband's close bond with his sister, the Queen, so her breaking with the Boleyns makes sense. If you were not for them, then you had to be against them, batting for the other side, the Lady Mary.

Sir Francis Bryan was one of the men who would help to bring about Anne's downfall. In 1536, when he and his friends were working against Anne, he visited Lady Rochford's father, Lord Morley. He may have gone to tell Morley that Lady Rochford had accused her husband and the Queen of incest. Bryan perhaps hoped to gain the support of the shocked father for the Lady Mary. He may have known that Morley was a friend of Mary.

With his wife and his daughter, Morley would visit Mary in June 1536. They spoke only of 'things touching to virtue'. Morley praised Mary in the books he gave her after that visit. When she became queen in 1553, he spoke of 'the love and truth that I have borne to your Highness from your childhood'. This shows he had been loyal to Mary long before June 1536.

Lady Rochford, it seems, had been swayed by her father's love for Princess Mary. Having been brought up at the court of Katherine of Aragon, she would have known Mary well. Lord Morley had held up the princess as a model of virtue and learning to his family. It is easy to see how Lady Rochford could have grown up loyal to Mary Tudor. It could be that she now saw herself as Mary's friend and hoped to see her named Henry's heir once more.

There was one other good reason why Lady Rochford could have come to hate the Boleyns in 1535. Her father had served the King's grandmother, the Lady Margaret Beaufort. In 1535, the Lady Margaret's great friend, the Bishop of Rochester, was put to death for being true to Queen Katherine. Lord Morley had been present in 1509 when Lady Margaret died during a Mass said by the Bishop. People blamed the Boleyns for the Bishop's fate, and it may well be that Lord Morley and his family did too. It seems that they, like so many others, had chosen to distance themselves from Anne and place their hopes for the future in the Lady Mary.

But in 1536, Lady Rochford went as far as to accuse her husband of incest with his sister, the Queen. Some writers have questioned this, but many sources of the time show that it was Lord Rochford's 'wicked wife' who betrayed this 'cursed secret' and was out for his blood. At his trial, Lord Rochford himself complained that he had been condemned on the word of 'only one woman'. What could have driven Lady Rochford to do that?

It seems their marriage was not happy. There were no children, though Lord Rochford had a bastard son. Rochford owned a book, an attack on women and marriage, that perhaps matched his own views on his wife. He had got it in 1526, within two years of his wedding, and the writer of the book dates his torments to the day he himself was wed.

Rochford had been at the royal court since his early teens at least. He was good-looking and loose in morals. Cavendish wrote that his life was 'not chaste', his 'living bestial'. He 'forced widows and maidens', and 'spared none at all'.

If he did not stop even at rape, then the word 'bestial' might well mean that he took part in buggery too. Cavendish refers to Rochford being unable to resist this 'vile' and 'unlawful deed'. On the scaffold, Rochford would confess that his sins were so shameful they were beyond belief, and he had known no man so evil.

Rochford may have forced his wife to submit to the kind of sex that outraged her. That was cause enough for her hatred. Some have said that Lady Rochford sought revenge on him after finding out that he had had gay sex with Mark Smeaton. But if that was true, why take it out on his sister Anne?

Lady Rochford may have been jealous of Rochford's close bond with Anne. It was said she 'acted more out of envy than out of love towards the King'. Perhaps she resented Anne for her part in getting her sent to the Tower. Or maybe she could see that the Boleyns were on a headlong course to ruin, and thought it a good idea to get on the right side of the King. It was wise to distance herself from the Queen's party at this time. And Cromwell, the King's chief minister, might have put pressure on her to speak against Anne.

Thanks to his wife, Lord Rochford was beheaded in May 1536. Lady Rochford, a 'widow in black' with a face of woe, left court. Her husband's assets were seized by the Crown and given away, leaving her very poor. Even her rich court gowns had been taken. She was forced to beg for help. The King acted at once, forcing Lord Rochford's father to give her a bigger income.

Soon after that, Lady Rochford was brought back to court as a lady-in-waiting to the next queen, Jane Seymour. She stayed in favour with the King, and was to serve two of his later wives, Anne of Cleves and Katherine Howard.

But in 1541, Lady Rochford became a party to treason. She rashly aided Katherine Howard's affair with Thomas Culpeper, helping them to meet in secret. She even let them use her own room at court. It was a stupid thing to do, and she was putting herself in grave danger. She has been called a meddler who got a sordid thrill from it all. Katherine Howard herself later accused Jane of having a 'wicked' mind. True or not, both acted like witless fools.

When Katherine's past came to light, she was put under guard with only Lady Rochford to wait on her. After the affair with Culpeper became known, Jane too was arrested. When Katherine went to Syon Abbey, Lady Rochford was sent to the Tower.

Some of the Queen's women told the council that Lady Rochford had been a party to a plot of the Queen's, and had passed on letters to Culpeper. They told how Lady Rochford had locked the King out that night, and how she had kept watch while Katherine and Culpeper brought each other to a climax. Then a letter from the Queen to her lover was found. 'Come to me when Lady Rochford be here,' she had written.

Lady Rochford was now seen as the chief cause of the Queen's folly. She, more than anyone, had good cause to know what became of people accused of treason. Quizzed by the council, she said she thought Culpeper had had sex with Queen Katherine. She told them that the affair had begun in the spring, and gave many details. She said that Katherine knew the risks she was taking. Culpeper, in turn, accused Lady Rochford of pressing him to love the Queen.

Back in her prison, 'that bawd Lady Rochford' was so scared of what might be done to her that, for a time, she was 'seized with raving madness'. The law did not permit mad persons to be put to death, but her 'fit of frenzy' did not save her. The King sent his doctors to treat her, and had an act act passed allowing him to put an insane traitor to death. In January 1542, Lady Rochford was found guilty of high treason, and she followed Katherine Howard to the block on 13 February 1542.

By the time Lady Rochford reached the scaffold, she was calm and ready to die. There was no sign of madness at her end. In her last speech, she spent a long time dwelling on her faults. She said that God had let her suffer this shameful doom, because she had helped to bring about her husband's death. 'I falsely accused him of loving his sister, Queen Anne Boleyn. For this I deserve to die. But I am guilty of no other crime.'

Jane, Lady Rochford, was buried, like most of the Tower's victims, in the royal chapel of St Peter. In 1876, experts dug up some of the graves, and some bones were found that they thought were hers. In fact, they were not her remains, and it is almost certain that the bones buried as 'Lady Rochford' were Anne Boleyn's.

Many years later, George Cavendish wrote that Lady Rochford's 'slander for ever shall be rife' and that she would be called the woman who craved vice. That is how she has gone down in history.

Chapter Six

Lady Jane Grey (1554)
The Nine-Days' Queen

A little over four hundred and fifty years ago, a girl of sixteen, Lady Jane Grey, was made Queen of England. She is famous because her reign was to last for only nine days, and she met a tragic end. She was the helpless victim of ruthless and greedy men. Of all the traitors of the Tower, her story is the saddest.

Jane was born in 1536, and perhaps named for Jane Seymour, the third wife of Henry VIII. Jane's mother, Frances Brandon, was Henry VIII's niece. Four years earlier, Frances had married Henry Grey, Lord Dorset. Jane was their eldest living child, but her sex was a bitter blow to her parents, who wanted a boy. Yet they knew she could be useful to them, for the royal blood of the Tudors ran in her veins.

In 1537, Jane Seymour died after giving Henry VIII the son he had long craved. The new prince was called Edward. For some years, Lady Jane Grey's parents plotted to marry her to him, and thus make her Queen of England in the future. That way, they could become a power in the land.

The Dorsets wanted Jane to be well taught. Their hopes of her were high. As soon as she was four, they arranged for her to have a tutor and be drilled in her lessons. They meant to make her a fit wife for a king. Jane was a clever child, very bright and able. Much was asked of her, but she did well in her studies, and grew to love her teachers.

Jane was a tiny girl, with fair, freckled skin and sandy red hair. She was plain rather than pretty, but that did not matter too much, because she was royal. All her life, her parents would look upon her as a pawn to be moved at their will. Worse still, they ill treated her badly in body and in spirit. They beat her and told her off for the slightest fault. They made her go hunting, which she hated. They dressed her in rich silks, but told her she would not go far on looks alone.

Two people brought some comfort to the young child. One was her kind nurse, Mrs Ellen. The other was her tutor, John Aylmer, who loved her and taught her to value learning for its own sake.

The happiest years of Jane's life were perhaps those she spent at court in the loving care of Henry VIII's sixth queen, Katherine Parr, who helped this clever and able child in her studies. Like John Aylmer, Katherine Parr was a staunch Protestant. Both of them may have inspired Jane to adopt the new faith, to which she stayed true all her life.

After Henry VIII died in 1547, his son Edward VI, then aged nine, became king and Jane went to live at Chelsea with the widowed Katherine Parr. Soon afterwards, Katherine married the charming and cunning Thomas, Lord Seymour, brother of the late Queen, Jane Seymour. Thomas Seymour now joined Lady Jane Grey's parents in plotting to marry her to the young King. He paid a lot of money to make her his ward, and told the Dorsets they would soon see their daughter Queen of England.

But Thomas Seymour had no power, and no way of bringing about the marriage. King Edward VI wanted to marry Mary, Queen of Scots, or a rich French princess. He was not interested in making Jane his wife.

Because King Edward was a child, England was then ruled by Thomas Seymour's brother, Lord Protector Somerset. Somerset found out about the plot to marry Jane to Edward, and was very angry with Seymour. Yet Jane was allowed to remain in Katherine Parr's household, and she must have been deeply upset when Katherine died in childbirth in 1548. Wearing a black gown, ten-year-old Jane acted as chief mourner when the Queen was buried at Sudeley Castle.

After that, she had to return home. Her parents wanted her brought up to be good, meek, sober and ready to obey them in all things, and she must have known what that meant. Her misery was clear to the famous tutor, Roger Ascham, who spoke with her at her family home when she was thirteen.

She told him, 'When I am with my father or mother, whether I speak, keep silent, sit, stand, eat, drink, be merry or sad, I must do it as perfectly as God made the world.' If she did not, she would be pinched, hit or worse. 'I think myself in hell,' she wept.

Under Edward VI, England had turned Protestant. The last years of the reign saw a growing gulf between Lady Jane Grey and the King's sister, Princess Mary, over matters of faith. Mary was a true Catholic, Jane a firm Protestant. In 1551, Jane visited Mary's house, New Hall in Essex, and there, in the chapel, saw a lady bow to the consecrated bread on the altar.

'Why do you do that?' Jane asked.

'I bow to Him that made us all,' the lady said.

'How can He that made us all be there, when the baker made Him?' Jane cried. Mary was shocked when she heard this. Yet she still tried to be friendly to Jane. She sent her a gown and some jewels. Jane would not wear them, as they were too rich. She now liked to wear sober black and white clothing, like a good Protestant girl.

By 1553, young King Edward VI was dying. Somerset was dead, and a mighty duke called John Dudley was ruling England in Edward's name. Dudley was making hasty plans to stop Mary from ever coming to the throne. He and Edward VI agreed that the claims of Mary Tudor and her sister Elizabeth should be passed over, and that the crown was to be left to Edward's cousin, Lady Jane Grey.

There were good reasons for this. Dudley wanted to remain in power. He could only do that if England had a monarch who would bow to his rule. Jane was the only member of the royal family who was likely to do that. But Jane proved not to be the meek little thing that Dudley thought her to be. She was a feisty, stubborn teenager, clever and candid, and not afraid to stand up to him.

Dudley had already got Jane's parents to agree

to a marriage between Jane and his son, Lord Guildford Dudley. Guildford was tall, fair and good-looking, but he was spoilt and surly. Jane did not want to marry at all. She wanted to be left alone with her books. She hated the Dudleys, and told her parents she would not have Guildford, but after being beaten by her mother, she had no choice but to agree. The marriage went ahead, but it was not a happy one. Jane refused to sleep with her husband. Nor would she name him king when the time came.

After Edward VI died in July 1553, Jane was brought to Syon House near London and there forced to agree to become Queen of England. When she saw all the court waiting for her, she began to shake with fright. Dudley led her to the throne and told her, to her horror, that Edward VI had named her his heir. As every person in the room knelt before her, Jane fainted. No one went to help her.

When she came to, she knew she must make a stand. She got up and said, 'The crown is not my right. It pleases me not. Mary is the rightful heir.' It did no good. Dudley, her parents and her husband Guildford forced her to do their will, and in the end, she had to give way. But she was not at peace with herself. She wrote later, 'It did not become me to accept.'

Soon afterwards, Jane was taken to the Tower of London to await her crowning. But her reign was to prove the shortest in English history. The people supported Mary, the rightful Queen. No one wanted Jane. As Mary was proclaimed queen, to the people's joy, Dudley was taken to the Tower. He was soon to die as a traitor.

Jane was at supper that day. She was aware of how quiet it was. Then her father ran in and tore down the royal arms above her chair.

'You are no longer queen,' he told her. She was not sorry to hear it.

'May I go home?' she asked. Her father did not answer, but fled from the Tower, leaving her to her fate. Soon, the guards came for her.

She was moved from the palace to the house of one of the jailers. They let her have books, and she lived in some comfort. She ate her meals with the jailer and his family. It was not a bad life, and she did not complain.

Jane had not wanted the throne, but in taking it she had been guilty of treason. Mary was right to fear that she would remain a focus for Protestant plots. So she kept her in the Tower, well looked after, but still a prisoner. She did not wish her harm, and meant to set her free one day, as soon as Mary herself had a son to be king after her.

Despite the Queen's wish to show mercy, Jane and Guildford were put on trial and sentenced to death. It was just for show, they were told. Mary would spare them the axe. 'It is believed Jane will not die,' wrote a courtier.

But Mary had restored the Catholic faith in England. She would burn those who did not accept it. She was planning to marry Philip of Spain, and the people did not want a foreign prince to rule over them. Early in 1554, Sir Thomas Wyatt led a major revolt against the marriage. Mary came close to losing her crown, but she made a brave stand, and the revolt was put down. It had been a near thing, and the council was in a panic.

Jane's father had been one of the rebel leaders, and had made it clear that he wanted his daughter Jane back on the throne. That was high treason. Jane knew nothing about it, nor had she had anything to do with the revolt. But that made no difference to those who thought she was a danger to Queen Mary.

Mary's lords now insisted that she put to death all who were a focus for any further revolt. It was made clear to her that Philip of Spain would not marry her unless Jane was 'removed'. Mary was in a corner. She had no choice in the matter, and a date was set for

Jane's sentence to be carried out. On being told she was to die, Jane said, 'I am ready and glad to end my woeful days.'

But Mary was deeply troubled about sending her young cousin to her death. She sent a priest to convert Jane to the Catholic faith. Jane was told that if she agreed, she might live. But she would not deny her Protestant God. 'It is not my desire to prolong my days,' she told the priest. He was moved by her faith, and asked if he could be with her at the end.

On 12 February 1554, Jane was ready to die. 'My soul will find mercy with God,' she wrote. Early in the day, ladies came to make sure she was not with child. If she had been, she would have been spared the axe, but she was not.

She put on a black dress and stood at the window. She had not agreed to see her husband Guildford to say farewell, but she had said she would watch him go to his death. She saw him weep as he walked under guard to Tower Hill. Not long afterwards, she saw a cart come back. It carried his bloody head and body, wrapped in white cloths. She cried out, 'Oh! How bitter is death!'

Now she saw the headsman on his return to the Tower. It was time.

On the arm of her jailer, Jane walked to the

scaffold. She was calm and brave. Her former nurse, Mrs Ellen, and her ladies came after, in floods of tears, and then the priest, keeping his promise. Jane climbed the steps and spoke to the crowd.

'Good people, I am come to die, by law,' she began. She said she had been guilty in taking the throne, but guiltless in never having wanted it. 'I die a true Christian woman,' she ended.

She asked the priest to join her in prayers, but he was too choked to reply. She kissed him goodbye as they held hands. The headsman tried to help her untie her gown, but she would not let him, and did it herself. He knelt, asking her to forgive him for what he must do, which she said she did.

It was now that she saw the block. He told her to stand in front of it.

'I pray you do it quickly,' she begged, and fell to her knees. 'Will you take it off before I lay me down?' She meant her head.

'No, Madam,' he said.

Jane bound her eyes and felt for the block. It was not there.

'What shall I do?' she cried in mounting panic. 'Where is it?'

No one moved as she groped in the air. Then

someone came and guided her hands. She laid her head down.

'Lord, into Thy hands I commend my spirit!' she cried. The axe came down. One witness wrote that he had never seen so much blood.

The headsman lifted the head.

'Behold the head of a traitor!' he called out.

Jane's remains, half naked, were left on the scaffold for some hours. Then she was buried in the chapel of St Peter, near her husband Guildford. Her father was beheaded not long afterwards, on Tower Hill. Her mother married again almost at once, and lived to see Elizabeth I come to the throne after Queen Mary died, in 1558.

Chapter Seven

Robert Devereux, Earl of Essex (1601) 'Strike Home!'

Robert Devereux was the son of the Earl of Essex. His mother Lettice was a cousin of Queen Elizabeth I, and had been called 'one of the best-looking ladies of the court'. For some months, Lettice had been having an affair with the Earl of Leicester. That had to be kept secret because she was married and Leicester was the Queen's great favourite. But Robert's father, the Earl of Essex, found out about the affair, and fell out with his wife and Leicester.

In 1576, Robert's father was serving in Ireland when he fell ill and died. At the end, he sent to Queen Elizabeth to ask her to 'be as a mother to my children'. His heir, Robert, was just nine when he became Earl of Essex after his father's death. He had been brought up in the house of William Cecil, the Queen's chief minister, and the Queen now put him under William Cecil's care.

In 1578, Robert's mother Lettice married the Earl of Leicester. Queen Elizabeth never quite forgave Leicester for this, and would not allow Lettice into her presence. In 1584, when Robert, Earl of Essex, was eighteen, Leicester brought him to court, where his good looks and manners 'won him the hearts of both Queen and people'. Yet it would be some time before Elizabeth came to see Essex as more than just a nice, polite boy.

In 1585, when Leicester led an army into Holland, Essex went with him as General of the Horse. He did so well in the jousts in honour of Leicester's coming that 'he gave all men hope he would be noble and forward in arms'. In 1586, he fought bravely in battle and was knighted by Leicester. They came back to England later that year.

Leicester returned to Holland in 1587 and, while he was away, Essex became closer to Queen Elizabeth. Essex was a good Protestant, with old royal blood in his veins. He was gallant, bold and generous, very tall, with reddish-brown hair and a beard. He wrote poems, was a good letter-writer and acted well in court plays. Women loved him.

Elizabeth found him charming and wanted him with her all the time. She knew he was not wise in state matters, but in other ways he was her idea of the perfect man. They went for walks and rides by day, and played cards all night to the sound of music.

By then Elizabeth was fifty-three, thirty-three years older than Essex, but that did not stop him paying court to her and acting as if he were in awe of her looks. The Queen thrived on his praise, as she had put about the myth that her beauty would never die, but she was now wearing wigs and heavy make-up to maintain it. With Essex, she seemed to have regained her lost youth.

But there was a darker side to Essex. He could be moody, lordly, spoilt and sulky, and, in a temper, would act without thinking. He never hid his feelings, and it was said that 'he carries his love and his hatred on his face'. He was a dreamer who rushed through life. He slept around, like any other young buck of the court, but then went to church to think on his sins.

He wanted to be a leader of men, but he never had the money to make that dream come true. He lived well beyond his means, leaving the Queen to pay his debts. He wanted glory in the field of battle, but was too rash and careless to make a great commander.

Essex and the Queen were two strong people, and often clashed. There would be sharp words, then Essex would sulk. Elizabeth needed him more than he needed her, so she always gave in. He would not allow her to rule him. He even ordered her about, and she let him do it. People were amazed that he got away with such conduct. But Elizabeth drew a firm line at giving him the high office that he really wanted. Sparks flew, but he could not bully her into agreeing.

In 1588, after England drove off the Spanish Armada, Leicester died. Elizabeth was bowed with grief, and after a time she turned to Essex, who soon became the most favoured man at court. He was liked by the people, even to the point of making the Queen jealous. The chief minister, William Cecil, tried to take him under his wing and teach him state affairs, but Essex wanted to get to the top as fast as possible.

When Elizabeth smiled on other young men at court, Essex made scenes and picked fights with them. In 1589, he was keen to go with Sir Francis Drake to destroy the Spanish fleet, but Elizabeth forbade it. He went anyway, much to her fury. The attack failed, but it was Drake who felt the Queen's anger, not Essex, whom she forgave.

William Cecil's son Robert was now one of the leading men at court, but Essex hated him. The Cecils stood for peace and stable rule, while Essex and his friends wanted war with Spain and the glory it would bring. The two parties became bitter rivals.

In 1590, Essex married in secret. His bride was Frances Sidney. Elizabeth thought Frances was not good enough for him, and raged for two weeks when she found out. Clad in black, Essex staged a funeral at court to show he was in disgrace. After that, Elizabeth took him back into favour. Frances stayed in the background.

By 1593, Essex had shown himself useful in setting up a spy service for the Queen, and at last, in reward, she gave him a seat on the council. 'He is a new man,' it was said, 'and has given up his former tricks.' But by 1596, Essex was bored with state duties and seeking action. Again, Elizabeth sent English ships to destroy Spain's new fleet. Essex carried out a daring raid on the port of Cadiz, causing dreadful damage. When a thrilled Elizabeth heard of it, she wrote to Essex, 'You have made me famous.'

It was Essex whose fame was sung far and wide. He had proved himself a hero, and was the man of the moment. When he got home, he was given a joyous welcome. No one was more loved by the people.

Elizabeth was jealous. When Essex came to her, she did not hail him as a victor, but asked what profit and gain he had brought from Cadiz. He had to admit there was none, and she snapped at him.

In truth, she feared he was a danger to her, being so loved by the people, and time would prove her right. She was now growing tired of him, and he of her. During one of their rows, he turned his back on her, she boxed his ears, and he even drew his sword and made to attack her. Anyone else would have been sent to the Tower, but Elizabeth did nothing. She feared how Essex might react.

In 1599, Essex was sent to Ireland to deal with the rebel Earl of Tyrone. His mission was a failure. He did not obey the Queen's orders to take to the field, and instead made a shameful peace with Tyrone. Elizabeth had told him to stay where he was, but he deserted his army, and hurried home on horseback to explain himself to her.

When he arrived at Nonsuch Palace, he burst into the Queen's rooms. Elizabeth was without her wig and make-up, and not yet dressed. Essex saw before him an ugly old woman. Elizabeth could not forgive that either. Essex was put under arrest, but no one thought the Queen would keep him locked up for long.

But Elizabeth had now heard how Essex had dined with the rebel Tyrone after making peace. That was the ruin of Essex. Kept under house arrest for a time, he fell ill. When he felt better, he began forming a party of young lords who felt they should have high office at court, and that England should fight Spain again. They began plotting against the council. In February 1601, they had the play *Richard II* staged in London. In this play, a king is toppled from his throne. That was a step too far.

The council knew what was going on, and feared what Essex might do. They put him under guard in his London house, but Essex got out and met up with his friends. With two hundred men, they tried to raise support for a revolt in London, but failed. Essex was again arrested, and taken to the Tower on the Queen's orders. Elizabeth would not go to bed until her orders had been carried out. She now saw Essex for what he was, but for all her courage during the revolt, she was 'much wasted', would not change her clothes, and kept a sword by her for fear of attack.

On 19 February 1601, Essex and the other young men were tried in Westminster Hall. They were charged with plotting against the Queen's crown and life, and with other crimes. Essex stood there smiling, but not for long. He pleaded not guilty, and said he had wanted to force the Queen to get rid of Robert Cecil.

'Will any man be so simple to take this as less than treason?' asked Sir Francis Bacon, acting for the Crown. No man was. Essex was condemned to a traitor's death. He seemed unmoved, and said he would not fawn and beg for himself, but that he had meant no harm to the Queen.

Many thought that if Essex pleaded for mercy, Elizabeth would spare him, but his pride would not allow it. The Dean of Norwich was sent by the council to get him to admit his guilt, but to no effect. On the day after Essex's trial, Elizabeth signed his death warrant in a firm hand.

On 21 February, Essex's chaplain saw him in the Tower and painted a fearful picture of the hell that was waiting for him if he did not own up to his sins. Now Essex did break down, and said he would confess in full all his crimes. The council went to see him, and he told them he was the most vile traitor that England had ever known. He admitted that the Queen would never be safe while he lived. He went over all his misdeeds in detail.

Essex's wife begged Cecil to ask the Queen to spare her husband's life, but Elizabeth would not, as 'he himself had shown he was not worthy of it'. She did grant that he could die in private, not on the public scaffold.

On 23 February, the death warrant was brought to the Tower. After it came a message from the Queen, saying Essex was not to suffer until the next day. That night, she sent two hangmen to carry out the sentence. 'If one faint, the other may perform it for him.' Then she shut herself in her rooms and stayed there until it was all over.

In the early hours of 25 February 1601, a small group of people arrived at the Tower to watch Essex die. They sat on seats around the scaffold, which was in front of the House of Ordnance, as Anne Boleyn's scaffold had been. Aided by three churchmen, Essex was brought out at eight o'clock. He wore a black velvet gown and breeches and a black felt hat. He climbed the steps, took off his hat and bowed to those watching. Then he made his speech.

'My sins are more in number than the hairs on my head,' he said. 'I have been puffed up with pride.' He asked Christ to pardon him, and spoke of 'my last sin, this great, this bloody, this crying sin', which had brought him and his friends to ruin. 'I beseech God to forgive us, and to forgive it me, most wretched of all.' He ended by praying God to save the Queen, 'whose death I never meant'.

Now he took off his gown and ruff, and knelt by the block, saying aloud the Lord's Prayer and the Creed. The headsman knelt and asked Essex's pardon, which he gave. Essex rose, then bowed to the block and laid himself down over it. He said he would be ready when he held out his arms.

'Lord, into Thy hands I commend my spirit!' he cried, twisting his head to the side. Then he cried, 'Strike home!' and flung out his arms, still praying. It took three chops to cut off his head, but he seems to have been killed by the first, as his body did not move after it. The headsman swung the head up by the hair and shouted, 'God save the Queen!'

Essex's death was mourned by many of the common people, who made up songs about him, such as 'Sweet England's Pride is Gone'. But Elizabeth never showed any regret for sending Essex to the block, for she felt she had been just in doing so, and that her realm was safer without him. Yet she would always think of him with sadness. Until her own death in March 1603, she would wear a ring he had given her.

Three hundred years later, the writer and statesman, Lord Macaulay, would visit the chapel of St Peter in the Tower of London and gaze upon the altar pavement. Beneath it had been buried the bodies of six of those 'traitors' who had lost their heads in the Tower. Macaulay was much moved, and wrote, 'There is no sadder spot on Earth.'

Quick Reads

Short, sharp shots of entertainment

As fast and furious as an action film. As thrilling as a theme park ride. Quick Reads are short sharp shots of entertainment – brilliantly written books by bestselling authors and celebrities. Whether you're an avid reader who wants a quick fix or haven't picked up a book since school, sit back, relax and let Quick Reads inspire you.

We would like to thank all our partners in the Quick Reads project for their help and support:

Arts Council England
The Department for Business, Innovation and Skills
NIACE
unionlearn
National Book Tokens
The Reading Agency
National Literacy Trust
Welsh Books Council
Basic Skills Cymru, Welsh Assembly Government
The Big Plus Scotland
DELNI
NALA

Quick Reads would also like to thank the Department for Business, Innovation and Skills; Arts Council England and World Book Day for their sponsorship and NIACE for their outreach work.

Quick Reads is a World Book Day initiative.
www.quickreads.org.uk   www.worldbookday.com

Quick Reads

Books in the Quick Reads series

www.vintage-books.co.uk